MYstory

MYstory

A Journal for Teens

Copyright © 2018 The Leadership Program

All rights reserved.

Published by The Leadership Program, New York
tlpnyc.com

The Leadership Program
535 8th Avenue, Floor 16 New York, NY 10018

Design by Paul Barrett, Girl Friday Productions
and The Leadership Program

ISBN-13: 978-1-941916-14-8
ISBN-10: 1-941916-14-7
First Edition

Printed in the United States of America

Contents

Introduction

WELCOME TO THE *MYSTORY* JOURNAL

This journal is divided into seven themes. Feel free to travel through these themes in any order you choose:

- Identity: Who You Are
- People You Are Closest To: Friends and Family
- Body Image: How You See Yourself
- Relationships: Friendships and Romance
- Dreams: Where You Are Going
- Heritage or Tradition: Where You Come From
- Legacy: What Impact You Want to Leave on the World

We hope that using this journal to tell *your* story turns out to be an enjoyable and fulfilling journey of self-discovery.

Identity

1

1

What are three things that you want the world to know about you?

....

....

....

....

....

....

....

....

....

....

....

....

2

Do you have a favorite poem or quote? If so, what is it? If not, is there something that one of your friends or family members have said that sticks in your mind?

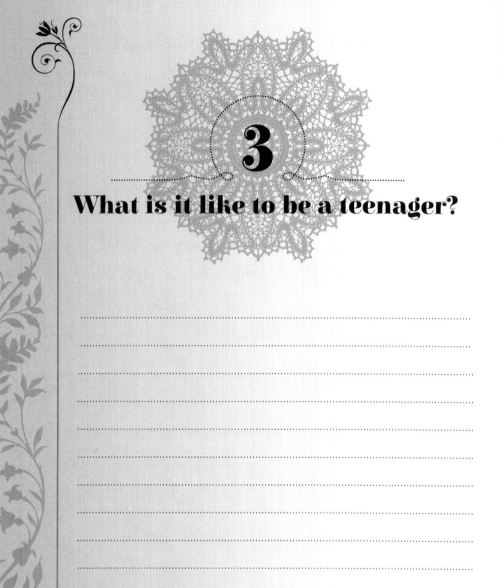

3

What is it like to be a teenager?

....
....
....
....
....
....
....
....
....
....
....
....
....
....
....
....
....

4

What is the best thing about being a teenager?

5

What is the worst thing about being a teenager?

6

Do people have expectations of you? If so, what are they?

7

How do you wish the world saw you?

....

....

....

....

....

....

....

....

....

....

....

....

....

....

What are some things that you think people say about you?

9

What are some things that you wish people would say about you?

....

....

....

....

....

....

....

....

....

....

....

....

....

....

....

10

What is something that you think you are good at?

11

What is something that you wish you were better at?

....
....
....
....
....
....
....
....
....
....
....
....
....
....

12

What do you think is the best part of your personality?

13

What is a part of your personality that you would like to improve?

....
....
....
....
....
....
....
....
....
....
....
....
....
....
....

People You Are Closest To

2

1

What kind of qualities do you look for in a friend?

What makes someone not just a friend, but a best friend?

3

Why do we need friends?

4

What are the most important things that your friends have taught you?

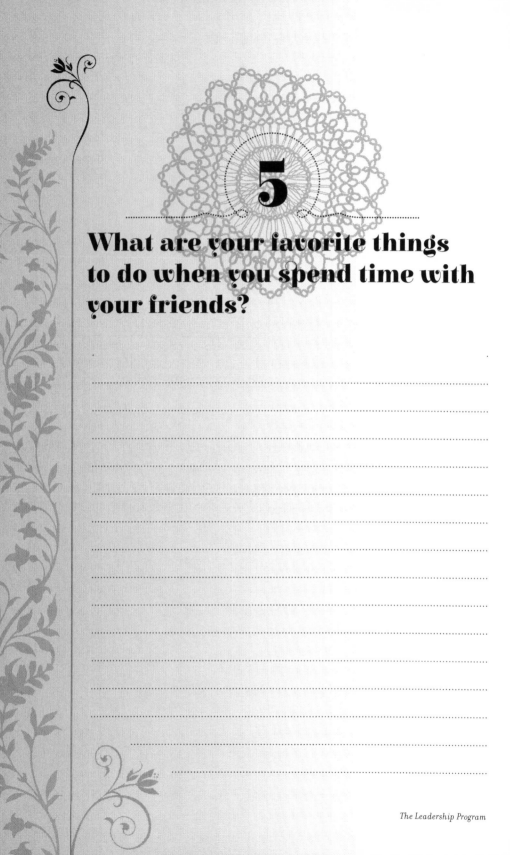

5

What are your favorite things to do when you spend time with your friends?

6

Have you ever been betrayed by a friend? How did it feel? How did you handle it?

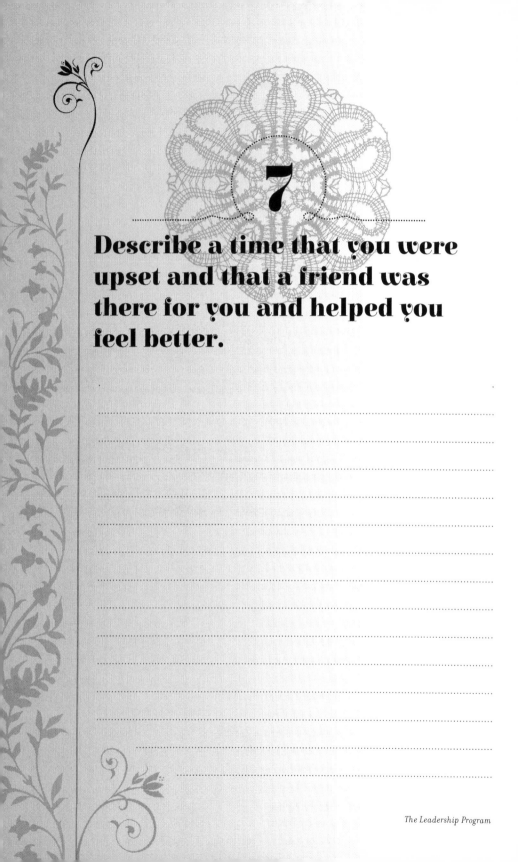

7

Describe a time that you were upset and that a friend was there for you and helped you feel better.

8

Use the space below to write any other feelings or stories you have about friends.

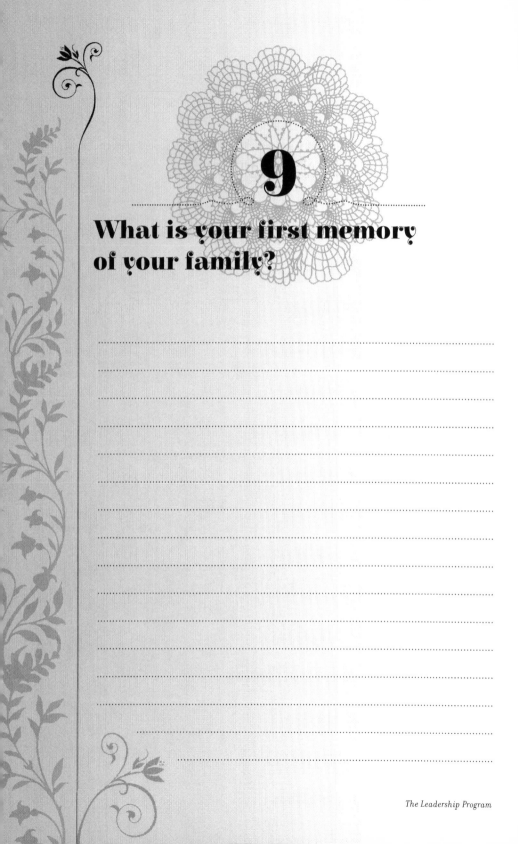

9

What is your first memory of your family?

10

Who are the most important members of your family today?

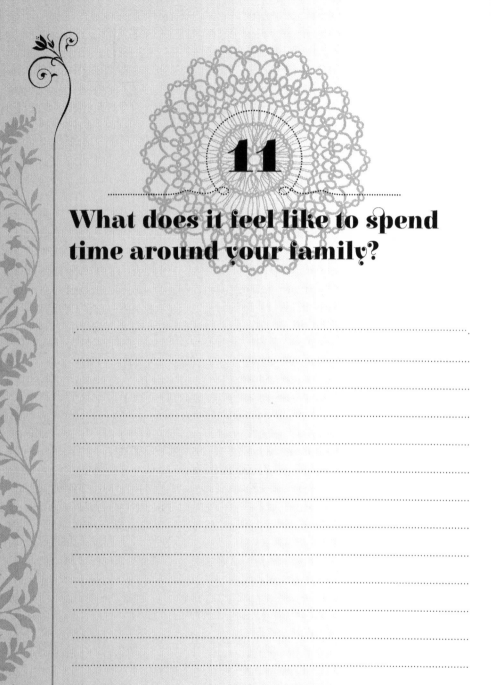

11

What does it feel like to spend time around your family?

....

....

....

....

....

....

....

....

....

....

....

....

....

....

....

....

....

12

What is the best thing about your family?

13

What is one thing about your family that you wish could be different?

14

Write a paragraph about an adult in your family with whom you are close. What is he or she like? How has this person been a role model to you?

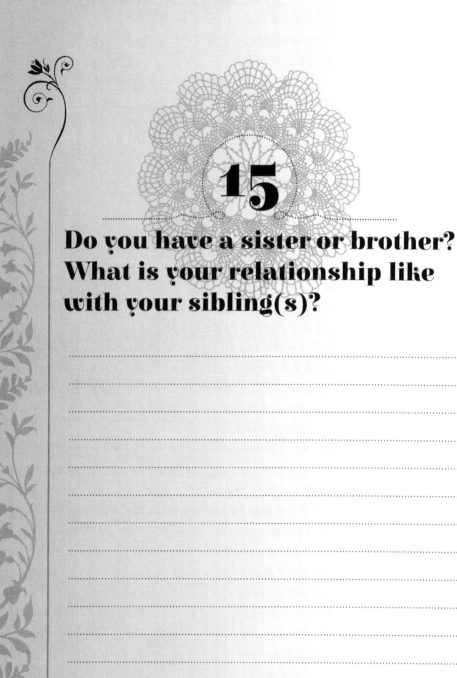

15

Do you have a sister or brother? What is your relationship like with your sibling(s)?

16

Is it important to have family? Why?

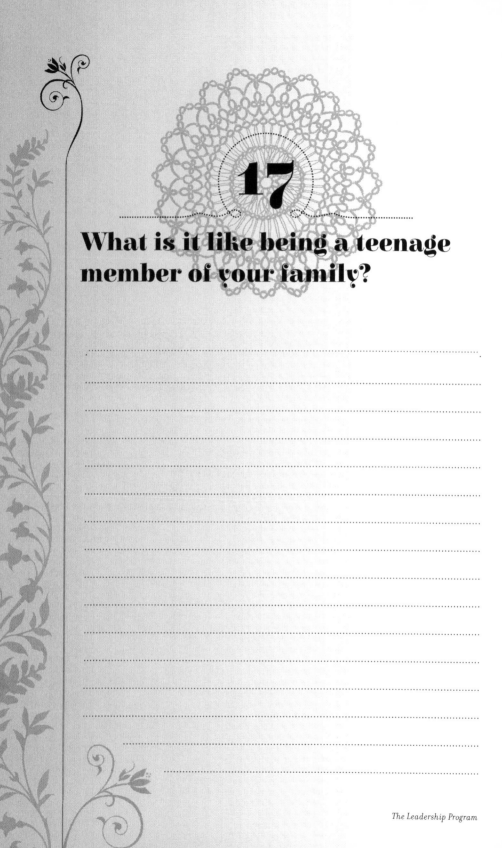

17

What is it like being a teenage member of your family?

Use the space below to write any other feelings or stories about the subject of family.

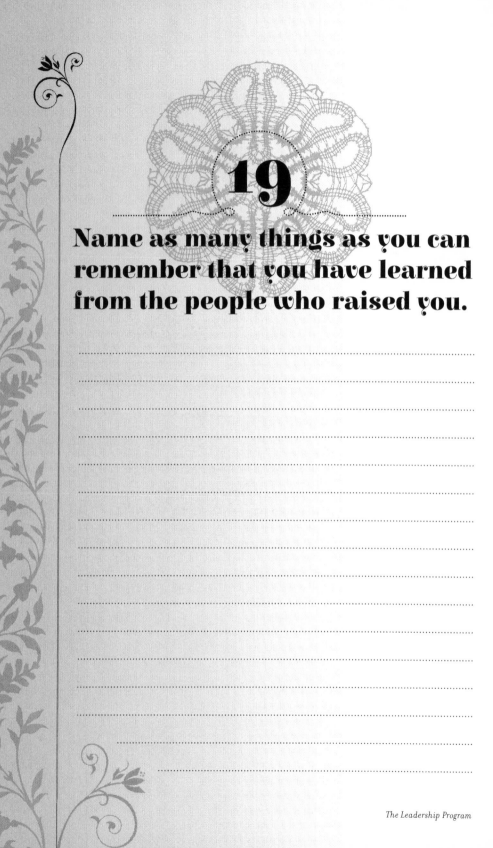

19

Name as many things as you can remember that you have learned from the people who raised you.

20

In what ways is your personality similar to that of others in your family?

21

In what ways are you different from others in your family?

....

....

....

....

....

....

....

....

....

....

....

....

....

....

What kind of dreams does your family have for you?

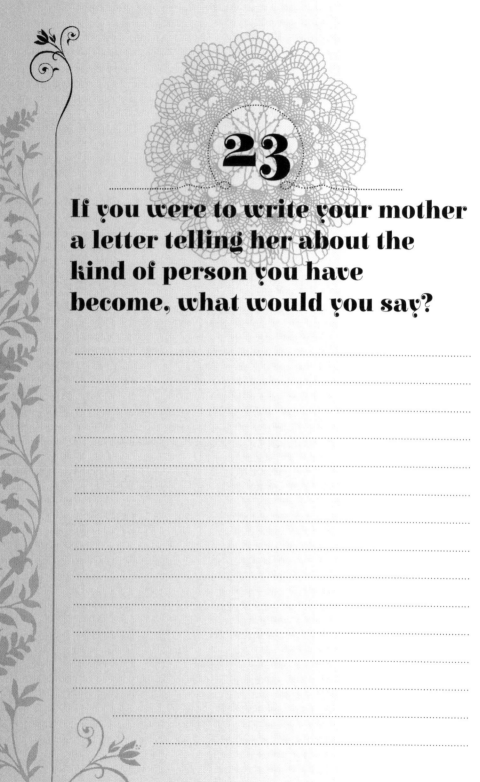

23

If you were to write your mother a letter telling her about the kind of person you have become, what would you say?

Do you have a role model? Who?
Why is she/he your role model?

25

What makes someone a good role model?

26

Write shout outs to two people who have helped you in your life.

27

Write two "R.I.P." shout-outs to anyone whom you loved and lost.

Body Image

3

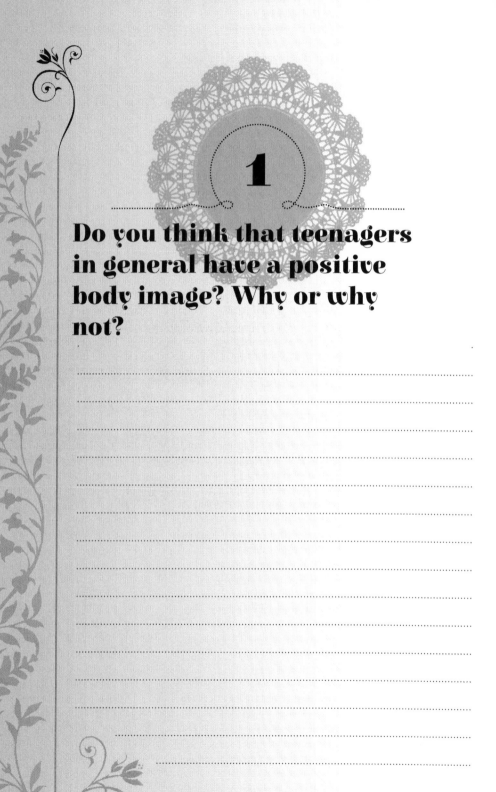

1

Do you think that teenagers in general have a positive body image? Why or why not?

....

....

....

....

....

....

....

....

....

....

....

....

....

....

2

Do you have a positive body image? Why or why not?

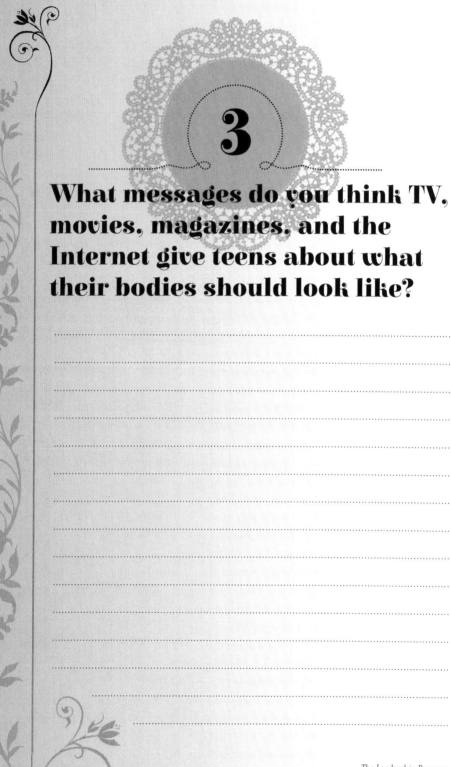

3

What messages do you think TV, movies, magazines, and the Internet give teens about what their bodies should look like?

....

....

....

....

....

....

....

....

....

....

....

....

....

....

....

What messages did/do you receive from your family about how you should look?

5

What messages do you receive from your friends about how you should look?

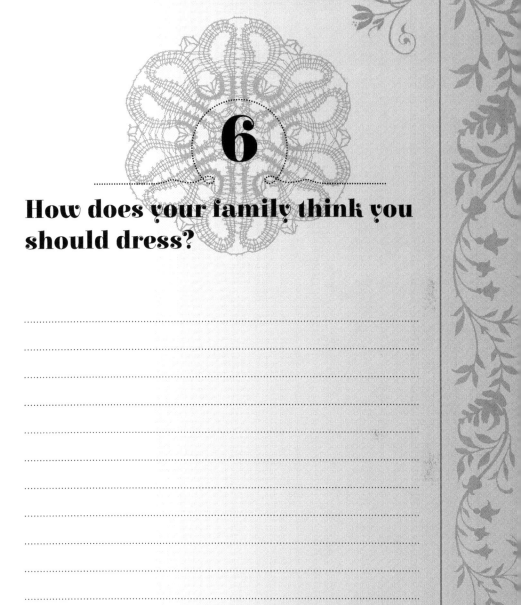

6

How does your family think you should dress?

7

How do your friends think you should dress?

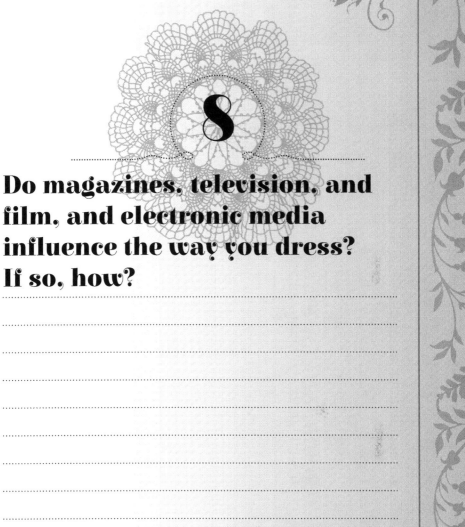

8

Do magazines, television, and film, and electronic media influence the way you dress? If so, how?

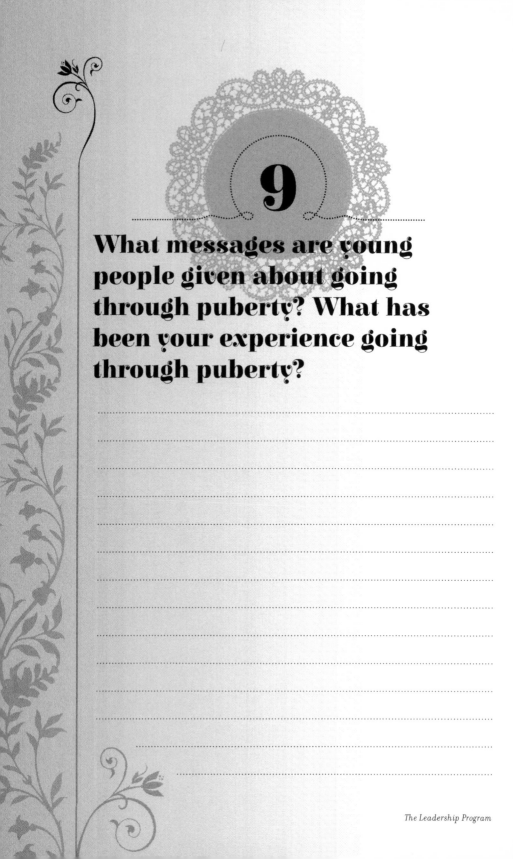

9

What messages are young people given about going through puberty? What has been your experience going through puberty?

10

What feelings come up when you think about your body? Why?

....
....
....
....
....
....
....
....
....
....
....
....
....
....
....
....
....
....

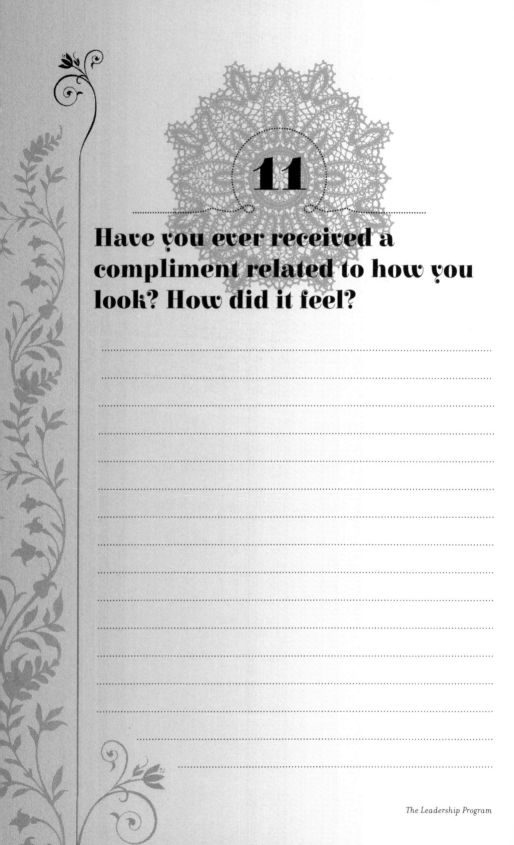

11

Have you ever received a compliment related to how you look? How did it feel?

12

Have you ever received an insult related to how you look? How did it feel?

....

....

....

....

....

....

....

....

....

....

....

....

....

....

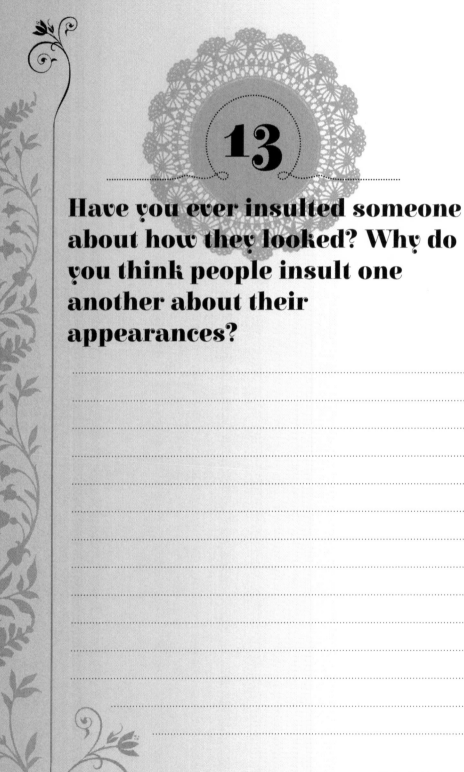

13

Have you ever insulted someone about how they looked? Why do you think people insult one another about their appearances?

List some compliments that teenage boys or girls might hear about their bodies.

....

....

....

....

....

....

....

....

....

....

....

....

....

....

15

List some insults that teenage boys or teenage girls might hear about their bodies.

Relationships

1

What did it feel like to have your first crush on someone?

2

Did you ever fight with one of your friends over a crush?

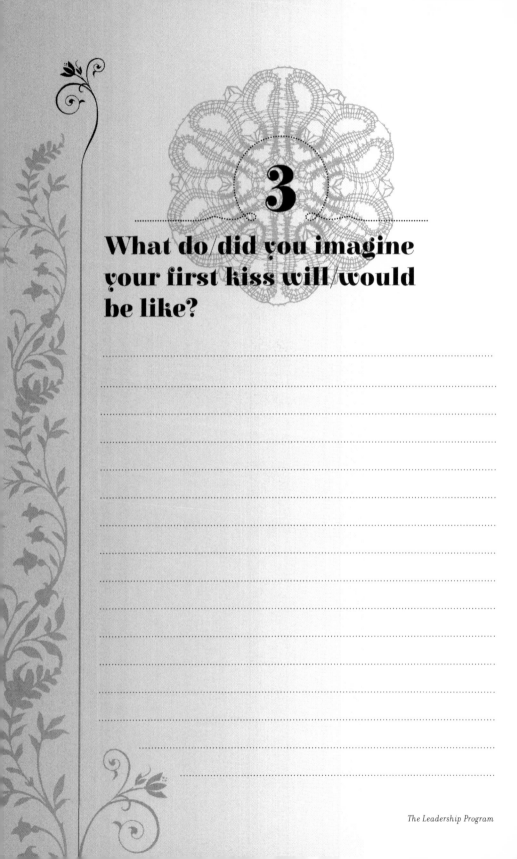

3

What do/did you imagine your first kiss will/would be like?

4

Have you ever had your heart broken or gone through a break-up? How did it feel?

5

What kind of romantic partner do you like?

6

Are you in love or have you ever been in love? How does it feel?

7

How do you think teenagers who identify as boys view girls?

....
....
....
....
....
....
....
....
....
....
....
....
....
....
....
....
....
....

How do you think teenagers who identify as girls view boys?

9

How do you think teenagers who identify as girls or boys view those who identify as gender non-conforming?

Dreams

1

What kind of dreams do you have for your future? What would you like to accomplish that you have not done yet?

What dreams does/did your family have for you?

....
....
....
....
....
....
....
....
....
....
....
....
....
....
....
....
....

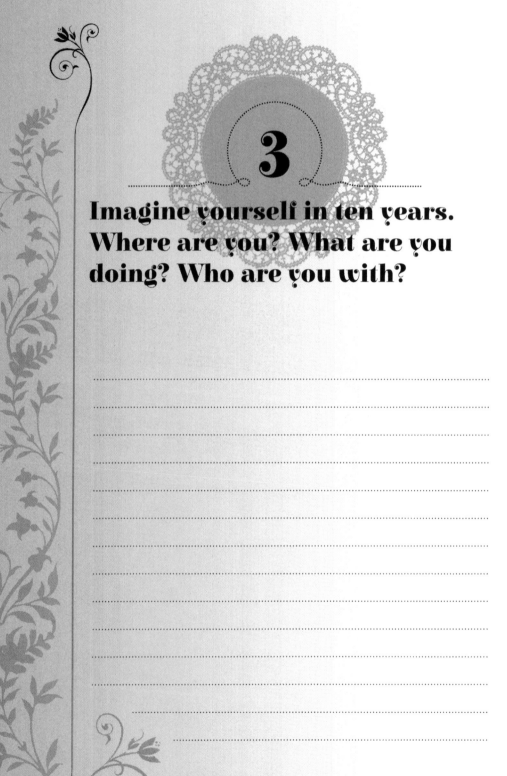

3

Imagine yourself in ten years. Where are you? What are you doing? Who are you with?

4

What kind of life do you dream about having?

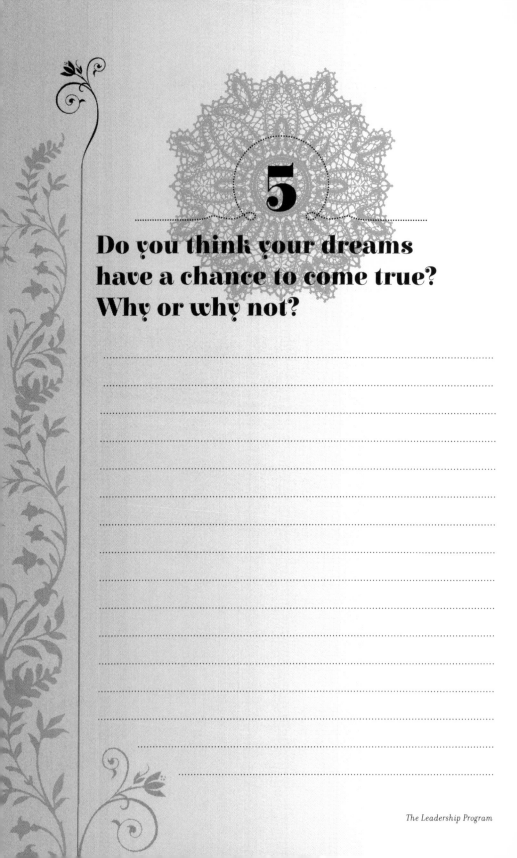

5

Do you think your dreams have a chance to come true? Why or why not?

6

What do you need to do to accomplish your dreams?

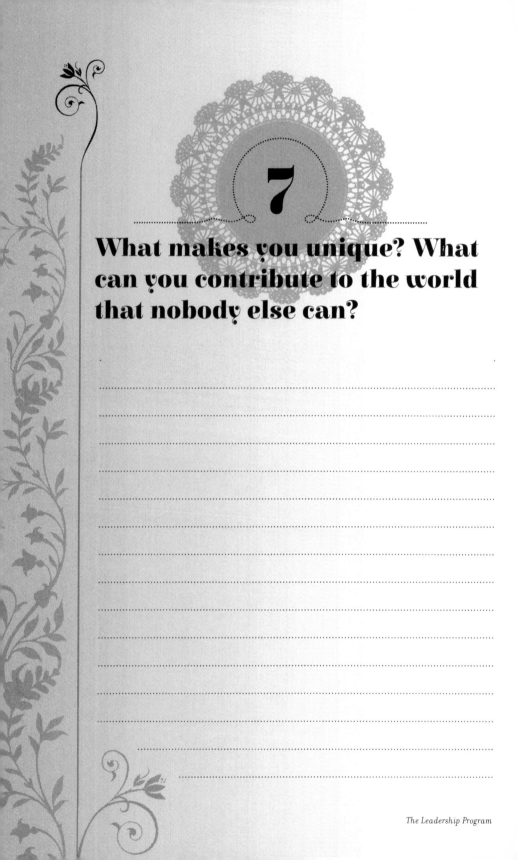

7

What makes you unique? What can you contribute to the world that nobody else can?

Who inspires you to keep following your dreams?

9

What advice would you give to young kids about following their dreams?

Heritage or Tradition

6

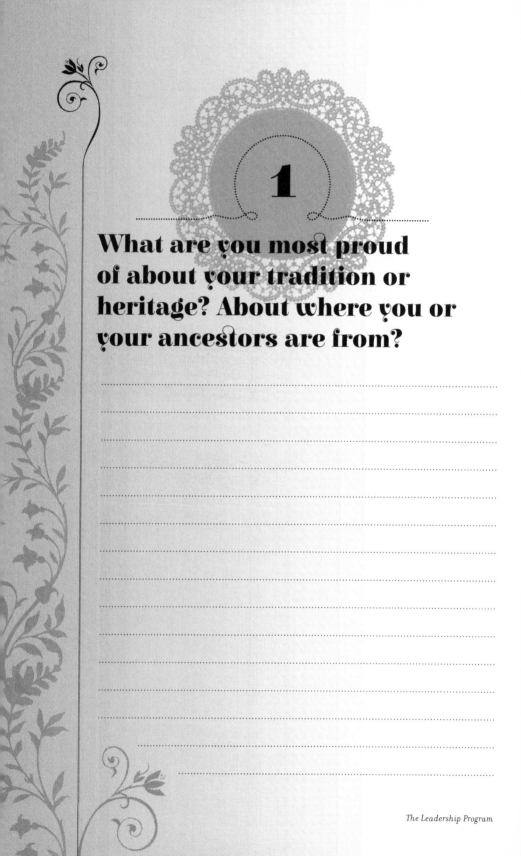

1

What are you most proud of about your tradition or heritage? About where you or your ancestors are from?

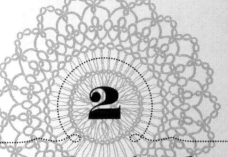

2

Describe your favorite place in the country from which your ancestors came, or your favorite thing about the art, music, or literature of your heritage or family tradition.

....
....
....
....
....
....
....
....
....
....
....
....
....
....

3

Describe some of your favorite food or recipes handed down from your ancestors or through family tradition.

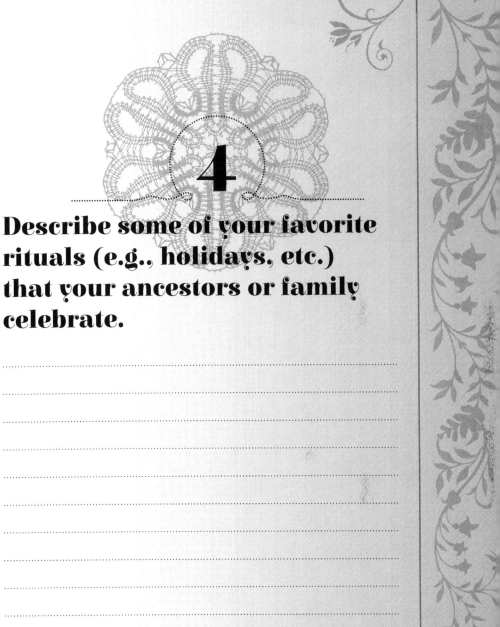

4

Describe some of your favorite rituals (e.g., holidays, etc.) that your ancestors or family celebrate.

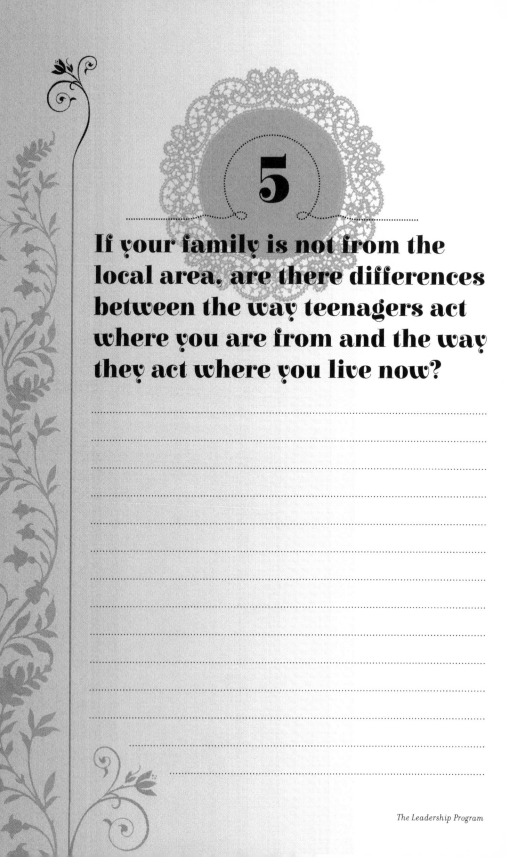

5

If your family is not from the local area, are there differences between the way teenagers act where you are from and the way they act where you live now?

6

Do our traditions or heritage affect who we are? How?

7

What would you like to teach people about your family traditions or your heritage?

Legacy

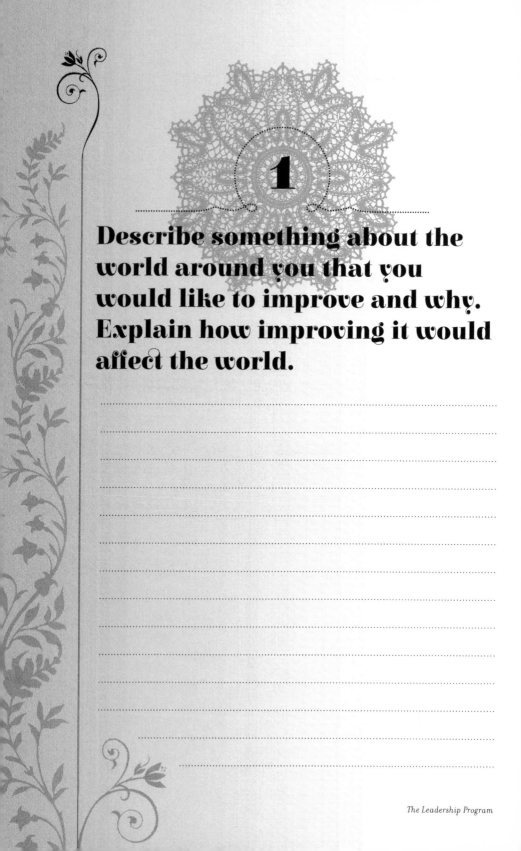

1

Describe something about the world around you that you would like to improve and why. Explain how improving it would affect the world.

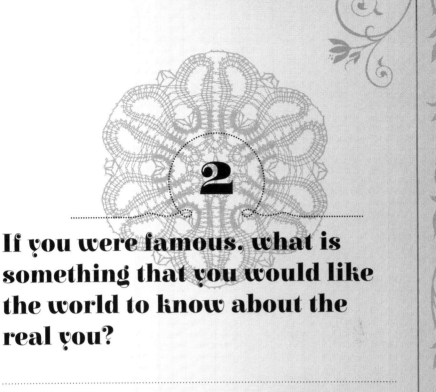

2

If you were famous, what is something that you would like the world to know about the real you?

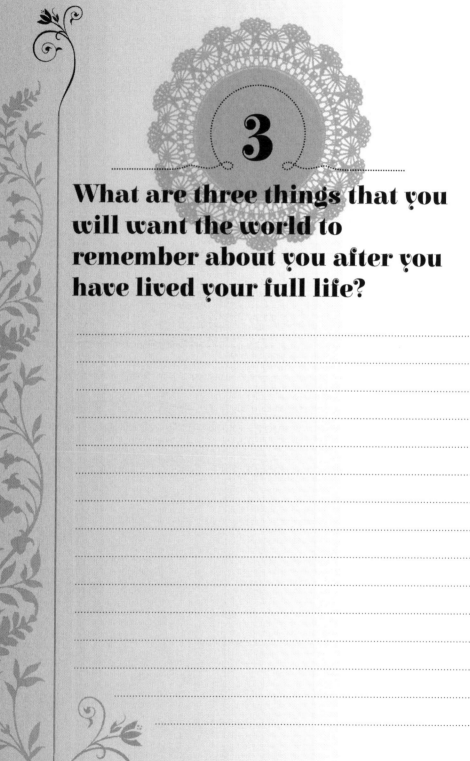

3

What are three things that you will want the world to remember about you after you have lived your full life?

4

Write a letter to your future grandchildren telling them in detail about the most important lessons that you have learned in life.

What does the word "legend" mean to you? What is a "personal legend"?

....
....
....
....
....
....
....
....
....
....
....
....
....

6

Create a poem that tells the story of why the world has never been the same since you came into it.

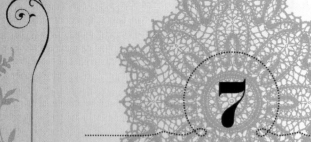

7

Explain why it is so important for teens to have a voice.

....
....
....
....
....
....
....
....
....
....
....
....
....
....
....
....

Write a poem about what it feels like to free your voice.

About The Leadership Program

OUR VISION

We create experiences that inspire people to step into their leadership and make positive change in their lives and in the world.

WHO WE ARE

For over twenty years, The Leadership Program has worked to provide youth development activities, as well as professional development and parent workshops and coaching.

The Leadership Program believes that with the right help, every person has the innate ability to lead the change.

Struggling with a goal? Feeling stuck creatively? Need inspiration? Whether it is personal development or professional grooming, we can get you there.

For more information about Leadership Program publications and programs, visit our website at tlpync.com or contact us at info@tlpnyc.com.

Made in the USA
Columbia, SC
15 December 2018